THRIVING IN COLLEGE

Ten Real World Lessons for College Success

RASHEEM ROOKE

WARBURTON
PUBLISHING

Copyright © 2025 by Rasheem Rooke

All rights reserved.

No part of this book may be reproduced in any form or by any electronic or mechanical means, including information storage and retrieval systems, without written permission from the author, except for the use of brief quotations in a book review.

ISBN
978-1-7363974-6-6

Dedication

To every student who has ever felt lost, uncertain, or unsure of what comes next.

This book is for you.

May it remind you that connecting the dots is possible, that your story is still being written, and that persistence will carry you further than you imagine. You are not alone on this journey. And your future is worth the work of finding the way.

CONTENTS

Preface	vii
Introduction	xi
1. The First 90 Days: Building the Foundation for College Success	1
2. Making Every Dollar Count: Understanding the Real Value of Scholarships	11
3. The Power of Connection: Building Your Support Network in College	19
4. Leading Without a Title: How Students Step Into Leadership From Day One	27
5. When Help Is Not the Same as a Handout: Understanding Emergency Student Aid and Unpaid Balances	35
6. Earning Without Burning Out: Balancing Work and College	43
7. Stronger Minds, Stronger Students: Why Mental Health is Academic Health	51
8. Beyond the Classroom: The Hidden Power of Internships and Experiential Learning	58
9. From Surviving to Thriving: Building Resilience in College Students	65
10. The Graduation Gap: Why Persistence Matters More Than Enrollment	72
11. Education as Transformation: Beyond the Degree	80
12. Study Guide: Discussion and Reflection Questions	86
About the Author	91
Also by Rasheem Rooke	93

PREFACE

Why I Wrote This Book

I started college with no safety net. At times, I was homeless and couch surfing, often hungry, and always unsure how I would make it through the week. My priorities were simple: survive today so I could get to tomorrow. Success in college wasn't at the top of my list... survival was.

My professional journey has always been rooted in education. My personal journey, not so much. Professionally, I began in student affairs and student support services, walking alongside college students as they learned how to find their place while in school. I later made a leap into the college access and scholarships space, helping students overcome the financial hurdles that often keep doors closed. Over the years, I also developed leadership programs that taught students that leadership is not about titles but about influence, service, and character. As I said, my professional journey has been rooted in education. But my personal journey was something completely different.

In my personal life, education was never the solid foundation it later became in my career. Growing up in a single-parent household and facing the daily realities of poverty, resources were scarce, and stability was often out of reach. I recall that in my junior year of high school, I had to leave home at 3:00 a.m. Walking from Yonkers, NY, to Mount Vernon, NY, because it was no longer physically safe to remain with my own mother. By the time I reached college, I was essentially on my own. I was an independent student with survival at the top of my priority list. College success, while meaningful, seemed distant compared to the immediate need to have food to eat, a safe place to sleep, and to manage life without a safety net. This meant I stumbled through my early college years as a below-average student, sometimes managing to be average at best. It wasn't until I discovered and began to utilize the resources around me, such as mentors, programs, and opportunities, that I learned how to shift from simply surviving to building a path toward thriving.

In each of the professional roles mentioned earlier, and upon reflecting on my own personal journey, I became clear on my understanding of higher education. Students were not leaving school because they lacked talent. They were leaving because they lacked guidance and support. A poor grade, an unpaid balance, an untreated mental health struggle, or a lack of belonging was enough to turn promise into disappointment. Families, if even present, often wanted to help but did not know how. Institutions sometimes created barriers without realizing it.

I realized that persistence, the ability to continue through challenges, was the missing piece of too many student stories. And persistence cannot be left to chance. It must be nurtured.

This book is my attempt to capture the lessons I have learned from my own experiences and the students, families, and colleagues who have shared their journeys with me. It is also a way to honor the resilience I have seen in college students who refused to quit, despite everything around them telling them to stop.

If you are a student, this book will help you see that you are not alone and will give you tools to keep going when the journey gets hard. If you are a parent or family member, it will help you understand how to guide and support without judgment or pressure. And if you are an institution, it will challenge you to think differently about the obstacles students face and the supports that make success possible.

You will not find theory here without practice. Every chapter combines stories with concrete steps. The aim is not just to inspire, but to equip. Students, families, and institutions each have a role to play in ensuring that enrollment leads to graduation.

I write this as a struggling college student who ultimately made it to graduation. I write this as a professional who has dedicated years to the success of students who were just like me. I write this for students who were high achievers in high school and are worried to death that they won't continue to succeed in college. But more importantly, I write this as someone who believes that education has the power to transform lives. A former supervisor of mine once told me that this is "liberation work," and I agree.

The chapters ahead are designed to illuminate the path, liberate students from negative thoughts that become obstacles to success, and position them to radically change their lives. This book will help students, families, and institutions on the journey from the first day of college to the last, so that more students not only survive higher education but thrive within it.

—Rasheem Rooke

INTRODUCTION

More Than a Degree: Why College Success Demands a New Conversation

When I first walked onto my college campus, I carried more worry than excitement. I worried about money. Looking at the academic calendar, I noticed that the dorms would close at the end of the semester, and I worried about finding an alternative place to sleep during the break. I worried about whether I even belonged there. My story was not unique. Thousands of students arrive at college each year with the same mix of hope and fear, full of promise but shadowed by obstacles that test persistence and resilience. Families celebrate enrollment as if it were the finish line, institutions tout recruitment numbers as proof of success, and students begin with high hopes of transformation. Yet too often, the story ends before the degree is conferred.

This book exists to change that story.

Through my work in higher education, student support services, college access, and scholarships, I have met thousands of students whose experiences reveal a truth we can no longer ignore: success in college is not automatic. And it does not depend only on intelligence or ambition. It is shaped by habits, networks, mental health, financial wisdom, and the ability to recover from setbacks, challenges, and obstacles. Degrees are earned not only in libraries and classrooms, but also in residence halls, counseling offices, career centers, student organizations, and family conversations late at night.

The chapters that follow are not abstract theories. They are practical lessons drawn from personal experience and professional insights gained from years of watching students navigate the gap between enrollment and graduation. They are written for three audiences at once:

- **Students**, who must make daily choices that determine persistence.
- **Families**, who serve as partners and encouragers in both triumph and struggle.
- **Institutions**, whose structures and policies can either open pathways or create barriers.

Each group of chapters builds on the last in a natural progression.

- **Chapters 1 through 3** focus on *laying the foundation*. These chapters cover the first-year experience, money management, and the importance of building networks early. Together, they provide students with the foundation they need to start strong.
- **Chapters 4 through 6** move into *growing skills and balance*. Here, the themes shift to leadership development, navigating aid and finances beyond scholarships, and balancing work commitments without losing focus.
- **Chapters 7 through 9** highlight the importance of *sustaining success*. These chapters address mental health, experiential learning, and resilience, which are the factors that help students maintain momentum through the middle years of college.

- **Chapter 10** closes with *the ultimate outcome*. It reminds us that the true measure of higher education is not enrollment, but persistence and graduation.

This structure is intentional. It mirrors the natural rhythm of the college experience: beginnings full of energy, growth through challenge, steadying oneself during difficult seasons, and ultimately crossing the finish line.

My hope is that this book will become more than just a resource. I hope it becomes a companion. For the student wondering if they belong, for the parent who wants to support without smothering, and for the college educator and administrator designing programs that matter, these pages offer guidance and encouragement.

A quick note: Because I have worked within and in partnership with well-known universities and organizations, the stories in this book reflect real experiences but not real names. To protect the privacy of the students whose journeys are shared, I have changed identifying details. What remains true are the lessons their stories reveal about persistence, resilience, and the real challenges of college success.

What also remains true... Enrollment is a door. Persistence is the path. Graduation is the goal. The journey between them is where transformation happens.

Let us begin.

Chapter One

THE FIRST 90 DAYS: BUILDING THE FOUNDATION FOR COLLEGE SUCCESS

The First 90 Days: Building the Foundation for College Success

The Beginning and Why the First 90 Days Matter

The first ninety days of college often carry more weight than any other stretch of time in a student's academic career. Families sometimes assume that the real measure of success will come at the end of the first year, or in the GPA that accumulates over four semesters. Others think the graduation stage four years later is the moment that matters most. Yet anyone who has spent years working with college students knows that the beginning shapes the end. The opening semester is not a trial period to be taken lightly. It is the foundation upon which everything else is built.

When students arrive on campus, they are surrounded by possibility. They bring with them dreams of careers, hopes for independence, and the pride of representing their families and communities. At the same time, they carry fears about whether they are ready, whether they will fit in, and whether they can manage the pressure. The transition is exhilarating but also fragile. The smallest decisions and the earliest experiences have the power to shape the trajectory of the entire journey.

I can trace the path of so many students back to these first weeks. A young woman who stepped into a leadership role during her freshman fall went on to graduate with honors and a resume filled with experiences that set her apart. Another student who never developed consistent study habits spent every semester scrambling and eventually gave up, convinced he was not cut out for higher education. The truth is that both students had the potential to succeed. What separated them was the foundation they built during those first ninety days.

The Importance of Belonging

At the heart of that foundation is belonging. Belonging is more than finding a few friends to sit with in the dining hall. It is about knowing that one's presence has value, that one is connected to something larger than themselves, and that there are people who will notice when they are absent. When a student feels that sense of connection, it becomes a buffer against the stress and disorientation that inevitably comes with college life.

One student I worked with joined the campus gospel choir within her first two weeks. She loved to sing, but she admitted later that she was mostly searching for a place where she would be accepted. That decision changed everything. The choir became her community. They prayed together, studied together, and supported one another in ways that went far beyond music. Whenever she faltered academically, someone from the choir encouraged her to keep going. She graduated not only because she worked hard but because she belonged.

Contrast that story with another student who never found his circle. He went to class, ate meals alone, and spent most evenings in his dorm room playing video games. By midterm, the loneliness had become heavy, and when he began to struggle in class, no one noticed. Despite my efforts, his story ended with a quiet withdrawal form I signed and an empty dorm room the following semester. He was bright, but brightness without belonging rarely lasts.

The research confirms what these stories illustrate. Students who do not feel connected within their first semester are far more likely to leave. Belonging is not optional. It is essential for success.

Academic Habits That Last

If belonging anchors students socially, habits anchor them academically. The routines established during the first semester often determine the academic rhythm for the remainder of the college years. This is when students decide whether they will attend classes consistently, whether they will prepare before lectures, and whether they will take responsibility for their learning.

Too many students arrive on campus assuming that college will be an extension of high school. They imagine they can skip classes without consequence, rely on last-minute cramming to carry them through exams, or submit assignments late for partial (or even full) credit. The reality is different. Faculty expect students to be curious, engaged, and present. Those who fall behind early often struggle to recover.

I recall a student named Carla who took my advice to heart. She decided during her first week that she would treat college like a full-time job. She attended every class, even the ones that seemed easy, and she set aside time every evening to review her notes. When exams came, she was never cramming. Instead, she was confident and prepared. Over the course of four years, her GPA never dipped below a 3.5, not because she was the most gifted student, but because she developed habits that worked.

On the other hand, I counseled a student who made a habit of skipping his eight a.m. lecture. He told himself that one missed class would not matter, but one became two, and soon he was relying on classmates for notes and missing key explanations. By the time midterms arrived, he was lost. His struggle was not a matter of intelligence but of habit. Once a poor routine takes hold, it becomes a difficult pattern to break.

The habits students form in those early weeks become the grooves in which the rest of their academic journey runs. Choosing to build strong routines early is an investment that pays dividends for years.

The Reality of Finances

Another truth about the first ninety days is that financial realities become clear. Many students arrive on campus with financial aid packages that look sufficient on paper, only to discover that books, food, transportation, and personal expenses quickly stretch their budgets beyond the breaking point. For some, this is the first time they are fully responsible for money management, and the learning curve is steep.

I once met a student who was juggling two part-time off-campus jobs by her second month on campus because she had underestimated her day-to-day expenses. She was working nearly thirty hours a week, which left her exhausted and unable to keep up with her coursework. Despite her determination, she eventually had to step back from school. What struck me most was that she had not been aware of the emergency aid fund that could have provided her with breathing room. Her story is not unusual. Too many students fall through financial cracks simply because they are unaware of available support.

Families and institutions must help students distinguish between everyday financial responsibilities and actual emergencies. Not every shortfall qualifies as a crisis, but when food insecurity, housing instability, or medical needs threaten persistence, students must know where to turn. For students, the first semester is the time to learn how to budget, how to ask questions, and how to seek guidance before small problems grow into insurmountable challenges.

The Role of Families

Families remain central during the first ninety days, though the relationship must shift. Students need independence, but they also need encouragement and perspective. Families who hover too closely risk suffocating growth, while families who disappear altogether risk leaving students adrift. The balance is delicate but achievable.

Parents who stay connected through weekly calls often provide a sense of stability, reminding students that they are not navigating this new world alone. Yet the most effective families are intentional about what they ask. Instead of focusing exclusively on grades, they inquire about friendships, professors, and campus involvement. These questions reinforce the importance of connection and engagement, not just academic performance.

One mother I spoke with made a habit of asking her daughter, "Who did you spend time with this week?" That simple question kept her daughter mindful of building relationships, which in turn anchored her socially and emotionally. Families can make a profound difference when they affirm that college success is about more than numbers on a transcript.

What Institutions Must Do

The responsibility for student success does not fall solely on students and families. Institutions have a critical role in shaping the first ninety days. Orientation is important, but a single weekend of programming is not enough to ensure retention. Having been responsible for planning and executing freshman orientation, I can tell you that institutions should count themselves fortunate if half of the freshman class even shows up. Support must continue throughout the semester in the form of mentoring, academic check-ins, and sustained opportunities for leadership development.

One of the most effective strategies I have seen is pairing first-year students with upper-class mentors who meet with them regularly. I've seen this work well at Howard University with their Campus Pals organization, where every incoming student was paired with a "campus pal." I have also seen it work at the rival Hampton University, less formally, with the "Bigs" (upper-classmen) and "Littles" (incoming freshmen). These relationships provide guidance, accountability, and encouragement during the most vulnerable months. Campuses that take the time to connect students in this way often see dramatic improvements in retention.

Equally important is the way institutions provide emergency aid. Too often, aid is viewed as a temporary solution for unpaid balances. When used intentionally, emergency aid addresses the crises that threaten persistence, such as food insecurity, housing, or access to healthcare. When a student knows that help is available in a moment of true need, they are more likely to push through rather than drop out.

Finally, institutions must take leadership development seriously from the first day. Students should not wait until junior year to be invited into leadership roles. Micro-opportunities, such as leading a small group project, coordinating a service event, or facilitating a study group, enable students to see themselves as contributors and change agents from an early stage. When students envision themselves as leaders, their commitment to the institution deepens.

Stories of Success and Struggle

Jordan arrived at college uncertain but eager. During orientation, he was paired with a peer mentor who guided him through his first semester. With encouragement, Jordan learned how to manage his time, developed strong study habits, and built confidence. His story illustrates what can happen when belonging, habits, and institutional support align.

By contrast, another student faced immediate financial pressure. She did not know how to budget and was unaware of the emergency aid resources available to her. By the middle of her second semester, she was forced to leave. Her story is a reminder that potential alone does not guarantee persistence. Without support and knowledge, students can slip away quietly.

Both Jordan and the other student were capable. The difference lay in the systems and choices that shaped their first ninety days.

Closing Reflections

The first ninety days of college are not a rehearsal. They are the performance that sets the stage for everything to come. Students who establish a sense of belonging, build strong habits, and learn to manage their finances in those early weeks are far more likely to persist. Families who provide balanced support and institutions that prioritize intentional programming amplify these chances even more.

The beginning matters because it contains the seeds of the end. When we invest in students during the first ninety days, we are not simply helping them survive the transition. We are laying the groundwork for graduation, for leadership, and for lives of purpose. The opening semester deserves our full attention, because when students thrive in the beginning, they are far more likely to thrive in the end.

Reflection and Practice

As you consider your own or your student's journey through the first ninety days, it is important to pause and apply the insights from this chapter. Reflection helps ideas take root. Practice turns them into habits.

Take time with the questions below. You may find it helpful to write in a journal, discuss with a mentor, or use them as conversation starters with your family. The goal is not simply to read but to act.

For Students

1. Think about the people you have met since arriving on campus. Who are the individuals who make you feel seen, supported, and valued? Write down their names and commit to reaching out to them on a regular basis.
2. Describe your current study routine. Are you attending classes consistently and reviewing notes soon after lectures, or are you waiting until exam time? What one adjustment could improve your routine this week?
3. Examine your spending over the past two weeks. Did it align with your budget, or do you even have a budget? What steps will you take to gain control of your finances before small leaks sink your ship?

For Families

1. How do you stay connected with your student? Reflect on the questions you ask. Are they focused solely on grades, or do they invite your student to share about friendships, mentors, and involvement?
2. Consider your response to financial concerns. Do you immediately send money, or do you help your student think through whether the issue is an emergency or an opportunity to practice budgeting?

For Institutions

1. Review your onboarding process. Does it extend beyond orientation? Are there intentional points of contact with first-year students throughout the semester?
2. Evaluate your emergency aid program. Does one exist? If so, does it target the issues that most directly threaten student persistence, or is it simply a tool to clear balances?
3. Look at your leadership offerings. How soon are students invited to take ownership, even in small ways?

Practice Steps

- **Students:** Schedule a visit with one professor during office hours this week, not to ask for help with a grade, but to introduce yourself individually, outside of class, and build a relationship.
- **Families:** Write down three supportive questions you can ask during your next conversation that go beyond grades.
- **Institutions:** Identify one new opportunity in the next month where first-year students can step into leadership, even in a small role.

Final Word

Reflection sharpens awareness, but practice builds change. If you are a student, your future self will thank you for the relationships, habits, and financial wisdom you put into place now. If you are a family member, your encouragement can be the difference between doubt and determination. If you are an educator or leader, the intentional steps you take to support first-year students have a ripple effect that extends into generations of graduates.

The first ninety days are not simply a season to endure. They serve as the launchpad for a college career. By choosing to reflect and act, you give yourself or your student the best possible chance not only to survive but to thrive.

Chapter Two

MAKING EVERY DOLLAR COUNT: UNDERSTANDING THE REAL VALUE OF SCHOLARSHIPS

Making Every Dollar Count: Understanding the Real Value of Scholarships

The Illusion of Arrival

For many students, the moment they are awarded a scholarship feels like arriving at the destination. Years of applications, essays, and waiting finally pay off. When that award letter or email arrives, students and families breathe a sigh of relief and assume the financial struggle is over. But in reality, this moment is not the end of the race; it is the beginning of a new one.

A scholarship is not a finish line. It is a tool, a resource, and a responsibility. And too often, students discover too late that treating it as a finish line leads to financial instability, unmet needs, and sometimes leaving school altogether.

Where Scholarships Really Go

One of the biggest misunderstandings about scholarships is where the money actually lands. Contrary to popular belief, most scholarships are not mailed as checks to students. They are sent to the college or university, where they are applied directly to tuition, fees, housing, or meal plans.

This structure ensures that the scholarship fulfills its intended purpose, which is to reduce educational costs. But it also creates a false sense of security. When tuition is zeroed out on a bill, students may believe they are financially set. What they fail to see are the costs that scholarships do not always cover, such as books, lab fees, transportation, personal expenses, or emergencies.

To make matters more complicated, scholarships often arrive as part of a broader package of financial aid. Federal and state grants, institutional scholarships, loans, and work-study programs often combine to cover costs. When these resources exceed the charges on a student's account, the extra money is often refunded to the student in cash. We will discuss this in a minute, but for many, that refund feels like free money. In reality, it is not free. It is part of a fragile balance of aid that must be stretched wisely.

Renewable or One-Time?

The next central question about any scholarship is whether it is renewable. Some awards are for one year only, designed to support a student's entry into college. Others renew automatically, but only if the student meets specific conditions, like maintaining a minimum GPA, completing a certain number of credits, or filing the FAFSA on time.

Too many students assume that once a scholarship is awarded, it will continue. I have watched oblivious students in their first year discover in their second year that their scholarship was not renewable. Without preparation, they turned to loans or dropped out entirely.

Smart students treat renewable scholarships as conditional resources, not guaranteed, but earned each year. They also plan ahead if a scholarship is nonrenewable, identifying how to replace those dollars through new applications, smaller local awards, or part-time work.

The Refund Temptation

Refund checks are another area where students often stumble. Imagine this scenario: a student's tuition and fees are fully covered by scholarships and grants. Once the school processes the aid, there is still a surplus. That money is deposited into the student's bank account.

For many, this is the first time they have ever held such a large sum. The temptation is enormous: new clothes, electronics, travel, or even lending money to friends. What is rarely considered are the necessities like textbooks, lab supplies, groceries, transportation, or emergency expenses that will arise later in the semester. By the time those needs appear, the refund has already been spent.

One student I met received nearly $2,000 as a refund at the start of her first semester. By October, it was gone. When her laptop crashed and she needed a replacement for class, she had no funds left. Her mother had to use a credit card to replace the student's laptop, causing the family's debt to grow. Another student, however, treated his refund as part of his budget. He separated the money into categories: books, personal expenses, and savings for emergencies. Then he lived within those limits. By the end of the year, he still had money left and no debt.

The difference was not in how much they received, but how they planned.

The Hidden Costs of College

Scholarships and grants are often designed to address the visible costs: tuition, housing, and meal plans. But college comes with a long list of hidden costs that can catch students off guard:

- Textbooks and lab manuals
- Equipment or technology upgrades
- Club and organization dues
- Professional clothing for internships or interviews
- Transportation to and from campus
- Healthcare and wellness expenses
- Personal emergencies

When students spend refund money recklessly or fail to account for these items, they are forced to scramble later in the semester. Budgeting for these hidden costs is one of the most overlooked but vital financial practices in college.

A Scholarship as Strategy

The students who succeed financially in college view scholarships not as one-time victories, but as tools within a broader financial strategy. They ask questions like:

- Is this award renewable, and under what conditions?
- What portion of my expenses does it cover, and what remains?
- How does this fit with my grants, loans, and work-study?
- How can I stretch refund money to cover hidden costs?

One student I worked with received a generous scholarship, but she didn't stop there. She applied for smaller community awards each year, tracked her GPA requirements carefully, and treated her refund as part of her semester budget. She worked a part-time campus job not because she had to, but because she wanted extra savings. By graduation, she had completed her degree with minimal debt and a cushion of savings for her transition into the workforce.

Her scholarship was not the finish line. It was a cornerstone in a carefully built plan.

Access and Success Are Not the Same

Perhaps the most important lesson about scholarships is this: access is not the same as success.

Scholarships create access. They allow students to enroll, sit in classrooms, and begin their journey. But success: graduation, personal growth, and career readiness, requires more than money. It requires persistence, resilience, and a web of support.

I have seen students celebrate the award as though the battle were won, only to falter in the months that followed. A scholarship covers tuition, but it does not guarantee good study habits, emotional well-being, or a sense of community. Success must be pursued intentionally.

Institutions and nonprofit organizations bear responsibility here. Awarding dollars is not enough. True investment requires wraparound support. It means offering mentorship, emergency aid, counseling, and leadership opportunities. It means checking in on students not only when tuition is due but when life gets hard.

I once met a student whose tuition was fully funded by a corporate donor. What kept her in school, however, was not the tuition check but the emergency grocery cards she received during a semester when her family could not send money. Another student told me that the leadership retreat funded by his scholarship program was the moment he began to see himself as capable of graduating. These supports transformed money into momentum.

Illustration: Think of a scholarship like a key to a locked door. Access means the student now has the key, but success means they walk through, explore the room, and eventually step into new opportunities beyond. Keys alone are not enough. Students need maps, companions, and guides once they enter.

For families, the lesson is simple: celebrate the scholarship, but do not assume it is enough. Ask what additional supports are available. For institutions, the message is urgent: dollars must be matched with intentional guidance. Otherwise, access risks becoming an unfinished story.

Closing Reflections

Scholarships change lives. They are powerful tools that open doors that might otherwise remain closed. But they are not the finish line. They are only the beginning.

Their true value lies not only in the dollars awarded but also in how those dollars are utilized. A scholarship on its own does not guarantee success. Managed wisely, it becomes part of a larger financial picture that includes grants, loans, work-study, and budgeting for the hidden costs of college life. Mismanaged or misunderstood, it can create a false sense of security that leaves students unprepared when expenses arise or funds run out.

Students must learn to view scholarships as instruments for long-term success, practicing financial literacy and planning for renewability. Families should celebrate the award while also encouraging their children to make disciplined choices. Institutions bear the responsibility of pairing every scholarship with the support systems that help students persist.

In the end, the measure of a scholarship is not the size of the check, but the degree earned, the opportunities seized, and the lives changed. A scholarship is not simply a reward. It is a responsibility. And when used wisely, it is one of the most powerful tools a student can have.

Reflection and Practice
    For Students

1. Ask whether your scholarship is renewable and what conditions apply.
2. Create a semester budget that includes hidden costs like supplies, transportation, and emergencies.
3. Treat refund checks as part of your financial plan, not as spending money.

For Families

1. Treat refund checks as part of your financial plan, not spending money.
2. Help your student think beyond year one and plan for renewability.
3. Encourage your student to apply for smaller, local scholarships each year.

For Institutions

1. Provide transparent communication about how scholarships and aid packages are structured.
2. Offer financial literacy workshops that include budgeting refund checks.
3. Support students in understanding the full scope of college costs, not just tuition.
4. Identify at least one partnership with community organizations that can provide additional wraparound services.

Practice Steps

- **Students:** Review your financial aid package and determine which scholarships are renewable. Build a simple budget that includes both refund checks and

hidden costs, and commit to tracking your spending for the first month of the semester.
- **Families:** Sit down with your student to discuss the renewability of their awards. Help them identify one practical way to use refund money wisely, such as saving for books, emergencies, or professional expenses.
- **Institutions:** Incorporate a financial literacy checkpoint into your scholarship program. This could be a required workshop or advising session that helps students understand renewability, refunds, and budgeting as part of their persistence plan.

Chapter Three

THE POWER OF CONNECTION: BUILDING YOUR SUPPORT NETWORK IN COLLEGE

The Power of Connection: Building Your Support Network in College

Why Networks Matter

College is often described as a journey, and like any journey, it is one that cannot be walked alone. Students may enter campus believing that academic ability alone will determine their success, but years of experience in higher education have shown me that this is not the case. Intelligence, talent, and even scholarships provide access, but support networks make persistence possible.

I have watched brilliant students leave school not because they lacked ability but because they felt isolated. I have seen others with average academic records thrive and graduate with honors because they surrounded themselves with people who encouraged, challenged, and supported them. The difference was rarely found in test scores or GPAs. The difference was found in networks.

Support networks in college are not optional. They are essential. They provide encouragement when doubt creeps in, direction when confusion arises, and stability when life feels uncertain. Networks act as both a cushion in moments of struggle and a springboard in moments of opportunity. In this chapter, we will explore the building blocks of these networks. Friends, faculty, and staff, as well as mentors and families, are cultivating the networks students need. This is the secret ingredient to thriving in college rather than simply surviving it.

Friends: The Peer Community That Shapes You

The first network most students form is with peers. Roommates, classmates, teammates, and members of student organizations often become the foundation of a student's daily life. Friendships in college matter not only because they provide companionship, but also because they shape behavior, motivation, and a sense of belonging.

I recall a student named Marcus, who was brilliant in the classroom but had a tendency to isolate himself. He went to class, returned to his room, and aside from visiting my office, spent most of his time alone. By the middle of the semester, he was overwhelmed and discouraged. When I asked about his circle of support, he admitted that he did not have one. His struggle was not about ability but about isolation.

Contrast his story with Danielle, who joined a cultural student organization during her first month. That community became her anchor. They studied together, celebrated together, and checked on one another. When Danielle considered dropping a class, her peers reminded her of her goals and encouraged her to push through. She later told me that without her friends, she would not have made it past her first year of college.

Friendships also provide accountability. Students who surround themselves with peers who attend class, complete assignments, and take their studies seriously are more likely to do the same. Students who fall in with circles where skipping class and ignoring responsibilities are normal often mirror that behavior. College friends are not just companions. They are mirrors, reflecting and reinforcing choices that can determine the path forward. The lesson is simple. Choose friends carefully. Seek peers who encourage growth and provide balance. The people who sit beside you in the dining hall or walk with you across campus may influence your future more than you realize.

Faculty and Staff: The Guides Who See Potential

While peers provide daily companionship, faculty and staff provide guidance that can transform the trajectory of a student's life. Professors, advisors, coaches, and program directors are more than authority figures. They are potential advocates, connectors, and mentors.

I once worked with a student who was the first in her family to attend college. She felt intimidated by professors and assumed that faculty were unapproachable. For weeks, she avoided speaking in class or attending office hours. Eventually, she gathered the courage to meet with one professor. That single meeting shifted everything. The professor not only clarified course material but also encouraged her to apply for a summer research program. She was accepted, gained valuable experience, and developed the confidence to pursue graduate school. All of it began with one relationship.

Another student, however, never built relationships with faculty. He sat in the back of classrooms, never asked questions, and avoided contact outside of lectures. When it came time to apply for internships, he had no one to write letters of recommendation. His lack of connection closed doors before they could open.

Faculty and staff notice students who show initiative. They often hold keys to opportunities that students do not even know exist. A recommendation from a professor, advice from an advisor, or encouragement from a staff member can propel a student forward in ways that money alone cannot. Students who learn to see faculty and staff as allies, rather than distant figures, discover a world of possibility.

The lesson here is that students must be intentional. Introduce yourself after class. Visit office hours. Say yes to opportunities to connect. Faculty and staff are not obstacles to be avoided. They are guides waiting to be invited into your journey.

Mentors: Wisdom for the Road Ahead

If friends provide companionship and faculty provide academic guidance, mentors provide perspective. Mentors are individuals who have walked the road ahead and offer wisdom, encouragement, and accountability. They may be alumni, professionals in a chosen field, or older students who have navigated similar challenges.

One of the most powerful stories I remember is of a student named Jamal. He connected with an alumnus who had once held the same leadership position in the same organization as Jamal. They began meeting monthly. The mentor helped Jamal think through not just his classes but also his long-term goals, professional development, and even personal struggles. Jamal often said that his mentor helped him see the bigger picture when stress made him lose focus. Their relationship lasted beyond graduation and became a lifelong bond.

By contrast, I recall another student who turned down opportunities to be matched with a mentor because he thought he could figure things out on his own. He later admitted that he felt lost navigating internships, networking, and career preparation. His academic performance was strong, but without guidance, he missed opportunities that could have shaped his future.

Mentorship accelerates growth. It allows students to learn from the experiences, mistakes, and successes of others. A good mentor does not remove challenges but helps a student face them with wisdom and resilience.

For institutions, creating structured mentorship programs can be transformational. When students are intentionally paired with mentors, retention rates improve, and student confidence grows. Mentorship is not about solving every problem but about ensuring that no student has to walk the road alone.

Family: The Anchor Beyond Campus

Even as students gain independence, family remains an essential part of the support network. Parents, guardians, siblings, and extended family members provide encouragement, perspective, and grounding. The challenge lies in finding the right balance between support and independence.

One mother I worked with called her daughter weekly, not to demand grades or pry into every detail, but to ask thoughtful questions like "Who are you spending time with?" and "What has inspired you this week?" Those conversations reminded her daughter that she was seen, valued, and supported. They became touchstones that anchored her during stressful seasons.

Another student, however, experienced the opposite. His family assumed that independence meant complete distance. They rarely checked in, and when they did, the conversations focused only on financial issues. He felt disconnected from home and carried the weight of college alone. That loneliness eventually eroded his motivation.

Families who strike the right balance empower students. They provide encouragement without suffocating growth, ask thoughtful questions without prying, and remind students of their worth without dictating their choices. A strong family connection remains a stabilizing force throughout the college journey.

Networks in Action: The Difference Between Surviving and Thriving

When we consider the layers of friends, faculty and staff, mentors, and family, we see how networks intertwine to create a web of support. Students who cultivate all four layers thrive. Those who neglect them struggle.

Take the story of Elena, a first-generation college student. She joined a peer study group, built relationships with professors, connected with a mentor through a campus resource, and maintained weekly calls with her family. Each of those networks provided strength at different points. Her peers held her accountable academically. Her professors opened doors to research. Her mentor guided her career path. Her family reminded her of her purpose. Elena not only graduated but went on to pursue graduate school with confidence.

But what about Jason? He relied solely on his scholarship funds and never invested in relationships. He avoided campus organizations, did not seek mentorship, and rarely spoke with professors. His family assumed he was independent and left him to his own devices. By his third semester, isolation had caught up with him. His grades slipped, and without anyone to encourage or guide him, he withdrew from school.

Both students entered with potential. The difference was not their intelligence or funding. The difference was their networks.

Closing Reflections

College is a collective endeavor. While it is the student who attends classes and completes assignments, success rarely happens in isolation. Networks provide the scaffolding that holds a student steady when challenges arise and lifts them higher when opportunities appear.

Friends offer companionship and accountability. Faculty and staff offer guidance and opportunity. Mentors offer wisdom and perspective. Families offer grounding and encouragement. Together, these networks form the ecosystem that makes thriving possible.

The truth is simple. Students cannot succeed alone. And they do not have to. The secret ingredient to thriving in college is not just effort or ability. It is connection.

Reflection and Practice
For Students

1. Reflect on your current circle of friends. Do they encourage your goals or distract you from them? What changes might you need to make?
2. Identify one professor or staff member you can introduce yourself to this week. What step will you take to build that relationship?
3. Consider whether you have a mentor. If not, who might you ask to fill that role?
4. Think about your connection with family. How can you keep them involved in a way that supports your growth?

For Families

1. How often do you connect with your student? Are your conversations balanced between academics, social life, and emotional well-being?
2. What questions can you ask that invite reflection rather than pressure?
3. How can you remind your student that they are valued beyond grades and performance?

For Institutions

1. Does your campus provide intentional opportunities for students to connect with peers?

2. Are faculty and staff encouraged to build relationships beyond the classroom?
3. Do you have structured mentorship programs, and if not, how can you create them?
4. How are families engaged in supporting student persistence?

Practice Steps

- **Students:** Schedule time with a professor or staff member this week to introduce yourself and ask one thoughtful question.
- **Families:** Write down three supportive questions you can ask your student that go beyond grades.
- **Institutions:** Identify one new program or initiative that could strengthen peer, faculty, or mentorship networks for first-year students.

Chapter Four

LEADING WITHOUT A TITLE: HOW STUDENTS STEP INTO LEADERSHIP FROM DAY ONE

Leading Without a Title: How Students Step Into Leadership From Day One

Rethinking Leadership

When most students think of leadership, they picture positions of authority. Student government president. Resident assistant. Club officer. Leadership is often reduced to titles printed on a resume. But leadership is bigger than that. It is about influence, service, and character.

Throughout my career in higher education and scholarship management, I have watched countless students miss opportunities to lead because they believed they had to wait for an official title. At the same time, I have seen others embrace leadership from their first day on campus, not because they were given authority, but because they recognized that leadership is a way of living.

The truth is that leadership does not require permission. It begins with the choices students make every day, in classrooms, in residence halls, and in communities. Titles may enhance a leader's reach, but they do not define leadership itself. In this chapter, we will explore how students can develop leadership skills from day one by focusing on influence, service, habits, and personal growth.

Leadership Is Influence, Not Authority

One of the most powerful lessons I have learned is that leadership begins with influence. Influence is the ability to shape outcomes, encourage others, and set an example. Authority may grant formal power, but influence earns trust.

I remember working with a student named Alexis who never held an official role on campus. She was not in student government, nor did she lead a club. Yet her peers constantly sought her out. Why? Because she listened. She encouraged them. She was the one who organized late-night study groups, reminded her friends of deadlines, and celebrated their achievements. Alexis had no title, but her influence was undeniable.

On the other hand, I recall a student who won a prominent campus leadership position but failed to connect with his peers. He spoke often about authority but rarely practiced empathy. Within months, he found himself isolated, his title carrying little weight. His experience revealed an important truth: authority without influence is empty.

Students must understand that influence comes before authority. Leadership is built on trust, consistency, and service long before it is recognized with a title. When influence comes first, authority, if it arrives, becomes more meaningful.

Everyday Leadership as Service

Another misconception about leadership is that it is about being in front. In reality, leadership is often about serving from within. True leaders notice needs, take initiative, and create solutions.

Consider the story of Ahmad, a sophomore who noticed that

many of his classmates struggled to find affordable textbooks. Instead of waiting for someone else to act, he created an informal book exchange program in his residence hall. Students began sharing books, saving money, and supporting one another. Ahmad never sought recognition. He simply served. Yet his initiative created a ripple effect that touched dozens of students.

Service is leadership because it models responsibility and care. Students who hold doors, tutor peers, volunteer in their communities, or help organize study groups are leading in ways that matter. These small acts accumulate into cultures of collaboration and compassion.

Institutions that encourage service as leadership help students reimagine what leadership looks like. A student does not need a microphone or a gavel to be a leader. They need eyes to see, ears to listen, and hands willing to act.

Habits That Prepare You Before Titles Arrive

Leadership is not an event. It is a collection of habits. Students who cultivate strong habits prepare themselves for leadership roles long before titles arrive.

One student I knew, Maya, consistently showed up early to meetings, completed tasks on time, and treated her peers with respect. She did not campaign for positions, but when opportunities arose, people naturally nominated her. Her habits spoke louder than her ambition. By the time she held a title, she was already recognized as a leader because she had been practicing it daily.

Contrast her story with another student who eagerly pursued a leadership role but failed to build habits of accountability. She arrived late to commitments, missed deadlines, and rarely followed through. When she finally earned a title, she struggled to fulfill the expectations. Without strong habits, titles crumble.

Habits like reliability, time management, empathy, and communication are the foundation of effective leadership. They may seem ordinary, but over time they build trust. When students consistently live out these habits, they lead without even realizing it.

Leadership in the Classroom

Leadership is not limited to student organizations or campus events. The classroom is one of the most overlooked arenas for leadership.

I once taught a freshman orientation class during a short stint at Lehman College, where a student named Bobby consistently modeled leadership by asking thoughtful questions, encouraging quieter peers to share, and respectfully challenging ideas. His presence elevated the class dynamic. He never announced himself as a leader, but others followed his example.

Leadership in the classroom looks like preparation, participation, and respect. Students who take initiative in discussions, help clarify assignments for peers, or communicate effectively with faculty demonstrate leadership. Their behavior shapes the learning environment for everyone.

Leadership Through Resilience

College inevitably brings challenges. Students will face setbacks, stress, and failure. How they respond to those challenges often reveals their leadership capacity.

I recall a student who lost her father during her sophomore year. She suddenly found herself responsible for covering expenses that had previously been secure. Instead of withdrawing or hiding her struggle, she reached out for help, shared her situation with faculty, and organized her schedule to balance work and school. Her resilience inspired her peers, who saw her not as a victim but as a model of perseverance.

Leadership through resilience is not about pretending everything is fine. It is about acknowledging difficulty, seeking support, and continuing forward. Students who respond to adversity with integrity and persistence lead by example, whether they realize it or not.

The Institutional Role in Developing Leaders

While leadership begins with students, institutions play a critical role in nurturing and recognizing it. Colleges that equate leadership only with formal positions risk overlooking the quiet leaders who shape culture every day.

At one university, a leadership development program required students to hold a formal title before they could participate. The result was predictable. The same group of highly visible students dominated the program year after year. Many potential leaders, especially those from marginalized communities, were excluded simply because they did not hold titles.

At Howard University, I took a different approach, creating the Bison Student Leadership Program. This program had a separate track that recognized and developed students who demonstrated leadership qualities regardless of position. Students were able to apply because they wanted to build habits, serve others, and grow their influence. Those students then participated in workshops, mentorship programs, and service-learning projects. The program uncovered leaders who might have otherwise been overlooked. One of those students later went on to serve as the student government president.

Institutions that broaden their definition of leadership empower more students to see themselves as capable. By valuing influence, service, and character alongside formal titles, colleges can create cultures where leadership flourishes in every corner of campus.

Stories of Leadership Without Titles

Sometimes the best way to understand leadership without a title is through stories.

- **The Peer Motivator:** A student named Carlos made it a habit to encourage his peers during exams. He sent motivational texts, organized group study sessions, and celebrated when others succeeded. He never sought recognition, but years later, his classmates still spoke of him as a leader.
- **The Silent Organizer:** Keisha, a quiet student, noticed that her club often struggled to plan events. She created a shared calendar, organized tasks, and helped keep the group on track. She rarely spoke in meetings, but her behind-the-scenes leadership held the group together.
- **The Courageous Advocate:** Tiffani experienced discrimination on campus and chose to speak up. She wrote op-eds in the student paper, organized dialogues, and collaborated with faculty to improve policies. She did not hold a position, but her advocacy reshaped the culture of her institution.

These stories remind us that leadership is not always loud or visible. It is often found in consistency, courage, and care.

Closing Reflections

Leadership is not reserved for those with titles. It is available to every student from the moment they step onto campus. Influence, service, habits, classroom presence, resilience, and advocacy all represent forms of leadership that shape communities and transform lives.

For students, the challenge is to embrace leadership now, not later. For families, the task is to encourage leadership in everyday choices, not just in visible achievements. For institutions, the

responsibility is to broaden the definition of leadership and create pathways for all students to grow.
The world does not need more titles. It needs more leaders. And leadership, at its core, begins with influence, integrity, and service.

Reflection and Practice
For Students

1. Reflect on the ways you have already led without realizing it. What small choices demonstrate leadership in your life?
2. Identify one act of service you can initiate this week that benefits others on your campus.
3. Consider your daily habits. Which of them strengthen your leadership, and which need to be changed?
4. Think about how you respond to challenges. How can resilience become part of your leadership identity?

For Families

1. Encourage your student to see leadership beyond titles. Celebrate acts of service, resilience, and influence.
2. Ask your student to share a recent example of when they positively influenced others.
3. Provide feedback that emphasizes character and habits rather than just achievements.

For Institutions

1. Review your leadership development programs. Do they include students without formal titles?

2. Create spaces where everyday leadership is recognized and nurtured.
3. Train faculty and staff to notice and affirm leadership in all its forms.
4. Ensure that leadership opportunities are accessible to students from diverse backgrounds.

Practice Steps

- **Students:** Commit to one habit this semester that reflects leadership, such as punctuality or consistent encouragement of peers.
- **Families:** Write a note to your student affirming a leadership quality you see in them.
- **Institutions:** Launch a recognition program that highlights "everyday leaders" on campus.

Chapter Five

WHEN HELP IS NOT THE SAME AS A HANDOUT: UNDERSTANDING EMERGENCY STUDENT AID AND UNPAID BALANCES

When Help Is Not the Same as a Handout: Understanding Emergency Student Aid and Unpaid Balances

A Misunderstood Lifeline

The call came late in the afternoon. A mother, her voice shaking, explained that her son had just been told he could not register for the upcoming semester because of an outstanding balance. She had heard about Emergency Student Aid through UNCF and assumed it was the solution. "Can he apply for that to cover what we owe?" she asked. Her question was not unusual. Many families assume that any kind of aid is designed to erase unpaid balances. But that is not what Emergency Student Aid was created to do.

Emergency Student Aid, often shortened to ESA, is designed to keep students enrolled when unexpected crises threaten their education. It is not a blanket solution for accumulated debt. The distinction may sound small, but it is critical. Confusing ESA with unpaid balance relief leads to disappointment, frustration, and missed opportunities. Families need clarity about what ESA can and cannot do, because misunderstanding it can mean the difference between a student staying in school or leaving.

In this chapter we will break down what ESA is, what unpaid balances are, why they are not interchangeable, and what families can do to help students navigate both. We will look at real stories, institutional perspectives, and practical steps to ensure that this misunderstood lifeline is used as it was intended.

What Emergency Student Aid Really Covers

ESA is designed for moments when life interrupts a student's ability to remain enrolled. Picture a student whose laptop is stolen the week before finals. Or another who suddenly loses housing because a roommate moves out and the lease becomes unaffordable. Or a student who needs emergency funds for a bus ticket home when a family member is ill. These are not theoretical scenarios. They are real-life emergencies that can derail progress if not addressed quickly.

I once worked with a student named Jackson, a sophomore who was thriving academically but juggling part-time work to make ends meet. One semester, his car broke down during midterms. Without reliable transportation, he couldn't get to his job or commute to campus, and within days, he was considering withdrawing. The repair cost was more than he could cover on his own, and missing work meant falling behind on rent. ESA provided a small grant to cover the repair, giving Jackson stability at a critical moment. That support allowed him to stay in class, keep his job, and continue toward graduation.

ESA is flexible, immediate, and targeted. It does not require long processing times or extensive applications. The goal is to solve a problem quickly, allowing the student to focus on school rather than survival. ESA is not about paying off accumulated tuition or longstanding bills. It is about addressing crises that, if left unresolved, would push students out of the classroom.

. . .

Why Unpaid Balances Are Different

Unpaid balances represent something else entirely. They accumulate when students owe tuition, housing, or fees from the current or previous semesters. These balances are often the result of gaps between financial aid and costs, changes in family income, or misunderstandings about billing. Unlike emergencies, unpaid balances are rarely sudden. They grow over time.

Consider the story of Jamal. By the end of his sophomore year, he owed more than four thousand dollars in unpaid tuition. His financial aid had covered most of his costs, but small gaps each semester added up. When his school placed a hold on his account, he could not register for classes. His mother hoped ESA would help, but the program was not designed for accumulated debt. What Jamal faced was a structural issue, not an emergency.

Unpaid balances are serious because they block progress and create difficult choices. Some students take on private loans at high interest rates. Others stop out of school with the hope of saving money to return. Still others leave permanently, carrying debt but no degree. Unlike emergencies, unpaid balances require long-term solutions, such as better financial planning, scholarship support, and institutional policy changes.

Why the Distinction Matters

When families confuse ESA with unpaid balance relief, frustration follows. Students request or apply for funds to which they are not eligible, parents become angry when applications are denied, and institutions are caught trying to explain a difference that feels technical but is actually fundamental.

The distinction matters because ESA is designed to be nimble, small, and immediate. If every unpaid balance qualified, the program would collapse under the weight of accumulated debt across thousands of students. By focusing only on true emergencies, ESA ensures that limited dollars can have maximum impact.

It also matters for student morale. When students believe ESA will wipe away debt and discover it cannot, they often feel betrayed. Clarity from the beginning avoids false hope and helps students seek the right solutions. Families who understand the difference can plan better, ask the right questions, and avoid disappointment.

Stories That Illustrate the Difference

To see the distinction clearly, let us look at three examples.

- **The True Emergency:** Maria's car broke down just as her internship was beginning. Without transportation, she risked losing both the internship and her financial aid eligibility tied to it. ESA provided funds for urgent repairs. Maria kept her internship and stayed enrolled.
- **The Accumulated Balance:** DeShawn carried a balance of fifteen hundred dollars from his first year. By his second year, the balance doubled because of unpaid fees and partial tuition gaps. He was blocked from registering. His family assumed ESA would help, but because this was not a sudden emergency, he did not qualify. The institution instead worked with him to explore a payment plan and identify scholarships for the next semester.
- **The Blurred Line:** Mikayla faced eviction from off-campus housing after her roommate left unexpectedly. While housing is often considered a long-term cost, her crisis was immediate. Without help, she would be homeless within weeks. ESA stepped in because the situation was urgent and unexpected. Her unpaid rent was not viewed as a balance owed to the institution,

but rather as an emergency that threatened her ability to stay in school.

These examples illustrate why ESA cannot be treated as a substitute for unpaid balance relief. Emergencies are sudden and immediate. Balances are cumulative and structural. Both are serious, but they require different tools.

What Students and Families Can Do

Understanding the distinction between ESA and unpaid balances is the first step. The next step is taking action.

For emergencies:

Students should know how to access ESA quickly. Keep the contact information for the financial aid office or the program manager handy. Do not wait until the problem spirals. If your laptop is stolen, your housing is disrupted, or you suddenly lack transportation, seek ESA immediately. It is designed for speed.

For unpaid balances:

Families must recognize that prevention is critical. Monitor your child's student account portal regularly. Ask student account professionals to explain charges in detail. If balances begin to accumulate, address them promptly before they become significant. Encourage students to apply for additional scholarships through platforms like opportunities.uncf.org. Explore work-study options. Above all, do not assume ESA will erase the problem.

For both emergencies and balances:

Communication is key. Students should keep their families informed about their financial standing. Families should ask open-ended questions like, "When have you looked at your student account last?" or "Is your balance paid, or are there any outstanding charges?" or "Have you noticed any new charges?" Early conversations prevent last-minute panic.

. . .

Institutional Perspectives

Institutions carry the responsibility of establishing and managing ESA with integrity while also supporting students with unpaid balances. The tension can be significant. On the one hand, staff want to help every student in need. On the other, ESA dollars are finite and must be reserved for emergencies.

At one HBCU, administrators created a clear communication strategy. Every time ESA was mentioned in an email or orientation session, they clarified that it did not apply to unpaid balances. They provided examples of eligible emergencies and shared resources for students struggling with long-term debt. As a result, confusion decreased, and families approached ESA with more realistic expectations.

Another institution, however, failed to make the distinction clear. Dozens of students applied for ESA to cover balances and were denied. Parents grew angry, accusing the school of being deceptive. The problem was not dishonesty but lack of clarity. Institutions that fail to define ESA precisely create unnecessary conflict and damage trust.

The best institutions combine ESA with other tools. They use ESA for true emergencies but also work with external scholarship resources, build their own scholarship funds, payment plans, and financial literacy programs to address unpaid balances. Students need both lifelines and long-term solutions.

Closing Reflections

Emergency Student Aid is a powerful tool, but it is not a cure-all. It is designed for crises, not for the slow accumulation of unpaid balances. The distinction matters because when ESA is used correctly, it keeps students enrolled during their most vulnerable moments. When it is misunderstood, disappointment follows.

Students and families who learn the difference are better prepared to navigate the financial realities of college. Institutions that communicate clearly build trust and prevent confusion. ESA is not a handout for debt. It is a lifeline in emergencies. Understanding that difference can be the key to persistence and graduation.

Reflection and Practice
For Students

1. Do you know how to access ESA on your campus? Write down the name of the office or the contact person responsible.
2. Reflect on the last semester. Did you face any emergencies that could have been addressed through ESA?
3. Review your student account online. Do you see any unpaid balances? If so, what steps can you take now to prevent them from growing?

For Families

1. Ask your student whether they know the difference between ESA and unpaid balances.
2. Discuss how you will handle unexpected crises. What resources will you explore before a problem becomes overwhelming?
3. Set a routine for checking student account statements together at least once per semester.

For Institutions

1. Does your institution provide ESA resources?
2. Are you communicating clearly about the purpose of ESA? Review your websites, emails, and orientation materials.

3. Do you provide examples of eligible emergencies and ineligible expenses?
4. What resources exist for students with unpaid balances, and how do you connect them to those resources?

Practice Steps

- **Students:** Create a list of three people or offices you can contact if you face an emergency this semester.
- **Families:** Commit to reviewing your student's account statement at the halfway point of each term.
- **Institutions:** Draft one email or handout that clearly explains the distinction between ESA and unpaid balances, and distribute it at the start of the next academic year.

Chapter Six

EARNING WITHOUT BURNING OUT: BALANCING WORK AND COLLEGE

Earning Without Burning Out: Balancing Work and College

The Double Life of College Students

It was just after midnight when I found myself talking with a student who had just finished working an evening program at our campus student center. His job was to set up and break down tables and chairs for events. He shared with me that he still had a paper due the next morning and an exam the following afternoon. His eyes were heavy, his hands shook slightly from fatigue, and yet he insisted, "I have to work. If I don't, I can't stay in school."

This conversation is not unusual. For many students, especially those from low-income backgrounds like myself, college is not just about lectures and study sessions. It is also about clocking in and out of jobs that keep tuition paid, bills covered, and food on the table. Nationally, millions of students balance employment and education, walking a tightrope between financial necessity and academic demands.

Work can be a blessing. It provides income, structure, and skills. But it can also be a burden if it tips into exhaustion, distraction, or missed opportunities. The difference lies in how students approach work, how families support them, and how institutions create systems that make balance possible.

This chapter explores the tension between working and studying. We will look at how students can earn without burning out, why certain jobs strengthen academic success, how overwork undermines persistence, and what institutions can do to help. Along the way, we will see stories of students who got it right and others who struggled, as well as lessons that every family and college can learn.

The Necessity of Work

The truth is that for many students, work is not optional. Tuition, housing, books, and everyday living expenses create gaps that scholarships and financial aid do not always fill. Families may contribute what they can, but rising costs often leave students with the responsibility to earn.

Consider Denise, a biology major who worked twenty hours per week at a campus library. The paycheck helped cover groceries and transportation, but it also gave her a sense of independence. She learned to manage her time, communicate with supervisors, and develop professional habits. Her job became a complement to her studies, not a competitor.

Now contrast her experience with Malik, who worked thirty-five hours a week at an off-campus restaurant. By the time he finished his shifts, he was too tired to focus on assignments. His grades slipped, he missed class regularly, and he felt disconnected from campus life. The income was necessary, but the cost was his academic performance.

Work can sustain, but it can also suffocate. The key lies in finding balance and knowing when work supports education and when it undermines it.

Choosing the Right Job

Not all jobs are created equal. Some jobs provide flexibility, proximity to campus, and opportunities for skill development that align with academic goals. Others demand long hours, late nights, or emotionally draining labor that interferes with coursework.

On-campus jobs often offer the greatest advantage. Supervisors in campus departments are more likely to understand academic schedules and provide flexibility during exams or midterms. Work-study positions, in particular, are designed to integrate employment with student success. Students in these roles often gain transferable skills, from data entry to event planning, that serve them long after graduation. I have personally seen students who worked as chairpersons of the campus homecoming committee go on to fruitful careers as event planners.

Off-campus jobs, while sometimes higher paying, can be more demanding. Long commutes, rigid schedules, and late-night shifts often clash with academic responsibilities. Students who must work off campus benefit from setting firm boundaries, such as limiting weekly hours or communicating openly with supervisors about class priorities.

I recall a student named Angela who intentionally sought a student assistant position in her department. The job not only provided income but also gave her hands-on experience that aligned with her career goals. By the time she graduated, she had both a degree and a resume filled with relevant work. Her job was not just about money. It was about momentum.

The lesson is clear. Whenever possible, students should pursue jobs that reinforce rather than compete with their education.

The Hidden Costs of Overwork

Students often underestimate the hidden costs of working too many hours. While the paycheck may provide short-term relief, the long-term impact can be devastating. Overwork leads to fatigue, missed classes, lower grades, and in many cases, dropping out altogether.

National data consistently show that students who work more than twenty hours per week are at higher risk of academic struggle. The math is simple. There are only so many hours in a day. Sleep, study, and social life cannot be endlessly compressed. Something gives, and too often it is academic performance.

Using myself as an example, I worked nearly full-time as front-desk security at a childcare center while enrolled in my second year of college. At first, I managed both work and school. But soon my grades declined, and I began skipping classes to catch up on sleep I missed while trying to balance both class and work. By the end of my second year, I faced academic probation, and I was on the verge of withdrawing. My story is not unusual. The paycheck seemed urgent, but the degree was far more valuable in the long run.

Students and families must recognize these trade-offs. A few extra dollars today are not worth the cost of lost momentum, delayed graduation, or dropping out altogether.

Building Time Management Skills

For students who must work, time management is the difference between thriving and burning out. Successful working students treat their schedules like contracts. They plan study hours, set aside rest, and protect time for academics with the same seriousness they give to work shifts.

Sophia, for example, balanced a twenty-hour per week job in the campus dining hall with a full course load. She carried a planner everywhere, blocking out specific hours for reading, assignments, and self-care. She rarely allowed work to bleed into academic time. Her structure gave her peace of mind and allowed her to succeed both on the job and in the classroom.

Institutions can help by offering workshops on time management, study skills, and balancing priorities. Families can encourage accountability by checking in not just on grades but also on routines. Students who learn to manage time well during college carry that skill into careers where competing priorities never disappear.

Institutional Responsibility

While students bear responsibility for balancing work and study, institutions play a crucial role in creating environments where balance is possible.

Colleges that offer robust on-campus employment opportunities provide students with the chance to earn while balancing their academics. Work-study programs, internships, and assistantships create pathways for income while supporting professional development.

Institutions can also provide emergency aid to reduce the need for excessive work. A small grant for books or housing may prevent a student from taking on additional shifts that would jeopardize coursework. Career services offices can connect students to part-time roles that align with their fields of study, making employment an extension of their learning experience.

The best institutions recognize that financial need and academic success are intertwined. They design systems that allow students to earn without burning out.

Families as Partners

Families may not always be able to reduce a student's need to work, but they can provide guidance and perspective. Too often, families encourage more hours because they equate work with responsibility. While the intention is good, the result can be harmful if it leads to exhaustion and failure.

Parents and guardians can help by asking thoughtful questions: "How many hours are you working?" "Are you able to keep up with your classes?" "Do you feel rested?" These questions acknowledge both financial and academic realities.

Families can also encourage students to prioritize long-term goals over short-term gains. A degree has far greater earning potential than a paycheck from part-time work. Supporting students in making wise choices about employment is an act of partnership in their success.

Closing Reflections

Balancing work and college is one of the greatest challenges students face. Work can be a source of growth, discipline, and financial stability. But it can also become a source of exhaustion, distraction, and derailment. The line between the two is thin, but it is navigable.

Students who choose jobs carefully, manage time well, and set boundaries can earn without burning out. Families who provide guidance and perspective can help students make wise choices. Institutions that create flexible, supportive employment opportunities can ensure that financial need does not become an obstacle to academic success.

The message is clear. Work and education do not have to compete. When balanced wisely, they can reinforce each other, creating graduates who are not only academically prepared but also professionally seasoned.

Reflection and Practice
For Students

1. Reflect on your current job. Does it support or compete with your academic goals? What changes might you need to make?
2. Track your weekly hours. Are you consistently working more than twenty hours? If so, how is it affecting your studies?
3. Identify one time management tool or strategy you can adopt this semester to protect academic time.

For Families

1. Ask your student how many hours they work each week and how it affects their rest and studies.
2. Discuss long-term goals. Remind them that the degree, not the paycheck, is the ultimate prize.
3. Encourage them to seek jobs that align with their academic or career interests.

For Institutions

1. Evaluate whether your campus provides sufficient on-campus job opportunities.
2. Consider how financial aid and emergency grants can reduce the need for excessive employment.
3. Train supervisors of student workers to understand the academic pressures students face and to provide flexibility when possible.

Practice Steps

- **Students:** Limit your weekly work hours to no more than twenty, and protect at least one full day each week for rest and study.

- **Families:** Schedule a check-in midway through the semester to discuss how work is affecting academics and well-being.
- **Institutions:** Expand or create a program that connects employment with professional development, such as research assistantships or skill-based internships.

Chapter Seven

STRONGER MINDS, STRONGER STUDENTS: WHY MENTAL HEALTH IS ACADEMIC HEALTH

Stronger Minds, Stronger Students: Why Mental Health Is Academic Health

When the Mind Shapes the Grade

A student once sat across from me in my office, eyes cast down, voice barely above a whisper. Her grades had plummeted, her professors were concerned, and she was on the verge of academic probation. On paper, she appeared to be a student who was not trying. In reality, she was carrying the weight of anxiety and depression that made even getting out of bed a monumental task.

This is the reality many students face. College is not just an academic experience. It is an emotional one. Success depends not only on knowledge and skills but also on mental health. A healthy mind creates the conditions for learning, resilience, and growth. A struggling mind can block even the most talented students from reaching their potential.

For too long, conversations about academic success have ignored the role of mental health. Families talk about grades, scholarships, and career paths, but not about stress, anxiety, or depression. Institutions focus on curriculum design and student engagement, but often fall short of providing adequate counseling and wellness support. Students themselves may downplay or deny their struggles, believing that asking for help is a sign of weakness.

The truth is simple. Mental health is academic health. In this chapter, we will explore why mental well-being matters as much as textbooks and lectures, how students can care for their minds, what families can do to support them, and how institutions can build environments where mental health is a priority, not an afterthought.

The Pressures Students Face

College brings incredible opportunities, but it also introduces significant pressures. Academic workload, financial stress, family expectations, and social challenges converge in ways that can overwhelm even the most prepared students.

Mario, a sophomore who excelled in high school. In college, he juggled a heavy course load, worked part-time, and felt pressure to make his family proud. Slowly, the weight became too much. He stopped sleeping well, skipped meals, and withdrew from his friends. His mental health deteriorated, and his grades followed.

This isn't an isolated incident. Surveys show that more than 60 percent of college students experience overwhelming anxiety, and nearly 40 percent report symptoms of depression during their academic career. These numbers are not abstract statistics. They are lived realities for students in every classroom and residence hall.

The pressures are not going away. If anything, they are increasing. Rising costs, social media comparison, and national and global uncertainty amplify the challenges. Students must learn not only how to manage their studies but also how to care for their minds.

. . .

Breaking the Stigma

One of the greatest barriers to addressing mental health is stigma. Many students, especially those from marginalized communities, have been taught that mental health struggles are a sign of weakness. Some believe that counseling is only for people in crisis. Others fear judgment from peers or family.

I remember a student named Alicia who resisted counseling even as she struggled with panic attacks. "I don't want people to think I'm broken," she confessed. After encouragement from a mentor, she finally visited the campus counseling center. The sessions helped her develop coping strategies, and she began to thrive again. Later, she said her only regret was waiting so long.

Breaking stigma requires courage and honesty. When students talk openly about their experiences, others feel less alone. When families acknowledge the importance of mental health, students feel permission to seek help. When institutions create campaigns that normalize counseling, students are more likely to use available resources.

The message must be clear: caring for mental health is not weakness. It is wisdom.

The Connection Between Mental Health and Academics

The link between mental health and academics is direct and undeniable. A student battling untreated depression may struggle with focus, memory, and motivation. Anxiety can make test-taking a nightmare. Stress can impair sleep, which affects learning and performance.

A student named Payton confided in me that she consistently underperformed on exams. After a candid conversation, she revealed that she experienced crippling test anxiety. We worked together to connect her with the counseling center, where she learned strategies to manage her anxiety. She then reported to me that her exam scores had improved, not because she had suddenly become smarter, but because she was finally able to demonstrate what she already knew.

When students prioritize their mental health, they create conditions that foster academic success. When institutions invest in counseling and wellness programs, they are not only serving students emotionally but also academically. Mental health is not separate from academics. It is foundational to it.

Building Healthy Habits

Students can take proactive steps to support their mental health. While counseling and therapy are essential for some, daily habits also play a critical role in maintaining well-being.

- **Sleep:** Students often sacrifice sleep to finish assignments or socialize. Yet adequate rest is one of the most important factors in mental health. Prioritizing seven to eight hours each night creates stability for both mood and cognition.
- **Nutrition:** Skipping meals or relying on fast food can harm mental health. Balanced meals stabilize energy and mood.
- **Exercise:** Even short bursts of physical activity reduce stress and improve mood.
- **Connection:** Isolation breeds distress. Building friendships, joining organizations, and seeking community provide protection against loneliness.
- **Mindfulness:** Practices like journaling, prayer, meditation, or deep breathing help students manage stress and remain grounded.

I once worked with a scholarship recipient who was struggling with anxiety. She began walking around campus each morning, leaving her phone behind. That simple habit cleared her mind, reduced her stress, and improved her focus. Sometimes small steps create powerful shifts.

The Role of Families

Families play a vital role in supporting student mental health. Parents and guardians often focus on grades or finances, but checking on emotional well-being is just as important.

I remember a mother who called her daughter every Sunday night to ask one question: "How is your heart?" That simple phrase opened space for her daughter to share joys, struggles, and worries. The conversations became a weekly lifeline.

Families can encourage students to use campus counseling services, normalize conversations about mental health, and look for warning signs such as withdrawal, irritability, or changes in sleep and appetite. They can also affirm that asking for help is not failure but strength.

When families create safe spaces for emotional honesty, students feel less alone in their struggles.

Institutional Responsibility

Institutions cannot treat mental health as an optional service. It must be a central priority.

Strong institutions invest in counseling centers, train faculty to recognize warning signs, empower peer counselors who advocate on behalf of their fellow students, and foster campus cultures that value wellness. They design schedules, policies, and support services with mental health in mind. For example, campuses that extend library hours during finals but also provide stress-reduction activities like yoga or therapy dogs show students that academics and wellness go hand in hand.

One university I came across embedded mental health education into first-year orientation. Every new student attended a session on recognizing stress, accessing counseling services, and establishing healthy routines. The results were striking. Students were more likely to use counseling services, and retention rates improved.

Institutions that neglect mental health pay a price. Students withdraw, retention declines, and academic outcomes suffer. Investing in wellness is not just compassionate. It is strategic.

Closing Reflections

Mental health is academic health. Students cannot thrive academically if they are struggling emotionally. Families cannot assume that grades tell the whole story. Institutions cannot ignore the reality that wellness drives persistence.

The good news is that change is possible. Students can develop healthy habits, seek help when needed, and support one another. Families can normalize conversations and encourage counseling. Institutions can prioritize mental health in their policies and practices.

Success in college is not measured only by grades or degrees. It is measured by the growth, resilience, and well-being of students. A diploma earned at the cost of mental health is no victory. A diploma earned alongside strong mental health is a true achievement.

Reflection and Practice
  For Students

1. Reflect on your current routines. Are you sleeping, eating, and exercising in ways that support your mental health?
2. Do you know where the counseling center is located and how to access it? If not, find out this week.
3. Who are three people on campus you can talk to when you feel stressed or overwhelmed?

For Families

1. How often do you ask your student about their emotional well-being, not just their academics?
2. What language can you use to normalize mental health conversations in your home?
3. If your student needed counseling, how would you encourage and support them in seeking it?

For Institutions

1. Do your policies and services reflect a commitment to mental health?
2. How accessible are your counseling centers, and are they staffed adequately?
3. How are faculty and staff trained to recognize and respond to signs of student distress?

Practice Steps

- **Students:** Commit to one new habit this week that supports mental health, such as consistent sleep or daily exercise.
- **Families:** Start one weekly check-in that focuses on your student's emotions, not just academics.
- **Institutions:** Launch one initiative this semester that explicitly connects mental health to academic success.

Chapter Eight

BEYOND THE CLASSROOM: THE HIDDEN POWER OF INTERNSHIPS AND EXPERIENTIAL LEARNING

Beyond the Classroom: The Hidden Power of Internships and Experiential Learning

Learning That Cannot Be Graded

Several years ago, I met a student named Tiana who carried a nearly perfect GPA. On paper, she appeared to be the ideal graduate. Yet when she applied for jobs, employers hesitated. She had the grades but no experience. Eventually, after months of rejection, she accepted an unpaid internship that gave her the skills and connections she lacked. Within weeks, she gained confidence, built a network, and secured a full-time offer after graduation.

Tiana's story reveals a truth that many students learn too late. A transcript, no matter how strong, is not enough. Employers want graduates who can demonstrate real-world skills, not just classroom knowledge. The bridge between theory and practice is built through internships and experiential learning.

In this chapter, we will explore why experiential learning matters, how students can maximize the benefits of internships, what families can do to support these opportunities, and how institutions can expand access to them. Along the way, we will hear stories of students who thrived because of hands-on experiences and those who struggled without them.

Why Internships Matter

Internships matter because they turn abstract concepts into lived skills. A student can study marketing theories for years, but until they pitch a campaign to a client, they do not fully understand how those theories apply in practice.

Kirk was an accounting major who spent a summer interning at a regional firm. He not only learned technical skills like preparing tax returns but also developed soft skills such as client communication and teamwork. When he returned to campus, his classes made more sense, and he had a clear vision of his career path.

Internships also create critical networks. Employers often hire from their intern pools because they have already tested the students in real-world environments. Many graduates secure their first jobs directly from internships. For first-generation students in particular, internships provide access to professional networks that family connections may not offer.

Internships are not optional extras. They are essential steps toward employment.

Experiential Learning Beyond Internships

While internships are the most visible form of experiential learning, they are not the only one. Service-learning projects, research assistantships, cooperative education programs, and even part-time jobs aligned with career goals all provide valuable experience.

For example, Maria, a psychology major, participated in a faculty-led research project examining adolescent behavior. She gained skills in data collection, analysis, and academic writing. By graduation, she had co-authored a paper, giving her a competitive edge in graduate school applications.

Another student, DeAndre, participated in a service-learning course where his class partnered with a local nonprofit. He developed grant-writing skills and built relationships with community leaders. The experience confirmed his passion for nonprofit management and provided material for his resume.

These experiences remind us that learning does not stop at the classroom door. Knowledge becomes powerful when it is applied.

The Cost Barrier

One of the most significant challenges with internships is cost. Many opportunities remain unpaid or underpaid, creating barriers for students who cannot afford to work without compensation. Students from wealthier families can accept unpaid internships in expensive cities, while low-income students are forced to decline. This creates inequities that follow students into the workforce.

I recall a student named Keisha who dreamed of working in publishing. She was offered an internship in New York, but the position was unpaid and housing costs were beyond her means. Without financial support, she declined the opportunity. Months later, she shared with me that several of her peers who accepted unpaid internships in the same field had secured jobs directly after graduation. Her lack of access had long-term consequences.

Institutions and families must recognize that financial barriers should not dictate opportunity. Scholarships, stipends, and creative solutions are needed to make experiential learning accessible to all.

Making the Most of an Internship

Securing an internship is only the first step. Making the most of it requires intentional effort. Students who thrive in internships do more than complete assigned tasks. They seek mentorship, ask questions, and take initiative.

Tyrell, a business major, began his internship quietly, waiting for instructions. After encouragement from his supervisor, he started volunteering for projects, scheduling informational interviews with colleagues, and presenting his own ideas. By the end of the summer, he was no longer just an intern. He was seen as a colleague. That distinction earned him a full-time offer.

Students should approach internships with curiosity and humility. Show up early. Take notes. Treat every assignment as important. Ask for feedback regularly. Build relationships, not just resumes. Internships are not simply about tasks completed. They are about building a reputation.

Families as Partners

Families play a crucial role in helping students appreciate the value of internships. Sometimes parents question why a student should take an unpaid or low-paid role when they could earn more in retail or food service. While financial concerns are real, families must weigh long-term benefits against short-term earnings.

A degree combined with experience often results in significantly higher lifetime earnings. Families who encourage students to pursue internships, even at temporary financial sacrifice, are investing in their future stability.

Families can also provide practical support, such as helping with transportation, providing meals, or offsetting costs when possible. Even small contributions can make internships feasible. Most importantly, families can celebrate the value of experience gained, not just dollars earned.

. . .

Institutional Responsibility

Institutions must do more to ensure equitable access to internships and experiential learning. Career services offices should build strong partnerships with employers, create pipelines for students, and provide resources for students to secure positions.

Some colleges have developed internship funds that provide stipends for unpaid or low-paid opportunities. Others have embedded experiential learning into graduation requirements, ensuring that every student, regardless of background, gains real-world experience.

One university I know of launched a "micro-internship" program, connecting students to short-term projects with alumni. These experiences required less time than traditional internships but still provided skills, networks, and references. The program was especially beneficial for students who could not relocate or work full-time during the summer.

Institutions that treat internships as central rather than optional demonstrate a commitment to student success beyond graduation.

Stories of Transformation

Imagine the following...

- **From Uncertain to Confident:** A student enters college unsure of her career path. Through a series of internships in marketing, she discovered her passion for digital media. By graduation, she not only had a degree but also a portfolio of work and a job waiting for her.
- **From Classroom to Career:** A computer science major joined a cooperative education program that alternated semesters of study with semesters of full-time employment. By the time he graduated, he had a

year of professional experience and multiple job offers.
- **From Struggle to Access:** A first-generation student, could not afford unpaid internships. Her institution provided a stipend that covered transportation and housing. That support enabled her to accept an opportunity that led directly to a job after graduation.

These stories show that internships and experiential learning do more than build resumes. They can change lives.

Closing Reflections

Internships and experiential learning are no longer optional in higher education. They are essential. Students who graduate without real-world experience face an uphill climb in the job market. Those who embrace opportunities early gain skills, confidence, and networks that set them apart.

The challenge is ensuring that all students, regardless of income or background, have access to these opportunities. Students must seek them, families must support them, and institutions must provide pathways that make them possible.

Education is not just about knowledge. It is about practice. Beyond the classroom lies the hidden power that transforms students from learners into professionals.

Reflection and Practice
For Students

1. Have you identified at least one internship or experiential learning opportunity aligned with your career goals?

2. How will you prepare to maximize the value of that experience?
3. What networks or mentors can you build during your next internship?

For Families

1. How can you support your student in pursuing internships, even if they are unpaid or low-paid?
2. What sacrifices might be worthwhile to secure long-term career benefits?
3. How will you celebrate the experience, not just the paycheck?

For Institutions

1. Do you provide stipends or scholarships for students who cannot afford unpaid internships?
2. How are you embedding experiential learning into curriculum and graduation requirements?
3. What partnerships with employers or alumni could expand opportunities for your students?

Practice Steps

- **Students:** Identify three potential internships or experiential learning opportunities this semester and apply for at least one.
- **Families:** Discuss with your student the long-term value of experience compared to short-term income.
- **Institutions:** Develop one new program or partnership this year that expands access to experiential learning for underserved students.

Chapter Nine

FROM SURVIVING TO THRIVING: BUILDING RESILIENCE IN COLLEGE STUDENTS

From Surviving to Thriving: Building Resilience in College Students

The Power of Bouncing Back

During my time as a student and my years working with students, I have often seen resilience become the deciding factor between those who graduated and those who did not. I remember one young man, Anthony, who faced setback after setback. His financial aid package was delayed. His laptop crashed during finals week. His part-time job unexpectedly reduced his hours. Each time, he adjusted, reached out for support, and kept moving forward. He was not untouched by hardship, but he refused to be undone by it.

That is resilience. It is not the absence of difficulty but the ability to respond, adapt, and keep going. College is filled with challenges like academic stress, financial strain, social pressures, and personal loss. Some students crumble under these pressures, while others develop the capacity to bend without breaking.

Resilience is not a mysterious trait that some people are born with and others are not. It is a skill that can be learned, practiced, and strengthened. In this chapter, we will explore what resilience looks like in the college environment, why it matters for persistence and graduation, and how students, families, and institutions can foster it.

Understanding Resilience

Resilience is the ability to recover quickly from setbacks and continue toward long-term goals despite obstacles. It is not about ignoring pain or pretending challenges do not exist. Instead, it is about finding the strength to face difficulties and the strategies to overcome them.

Psychologists often describe resilience as a combination of emotional regulation, problem-solving, and social support. Students who are resilient manage stress effectively, maintain perspective, and draw strength from their networks.

Elena was a first-generation student whose mother was hospitalized during her junior year. Elena missed classes, fell behind on assignments, and considered withdrawing. But with the support of her professors, counseling services, and family encouragement, she caught up and finished the semester. She did not avoid hardship… she overcame it.

Why Resilience Matters in College

Resilience is essential because college life guarantees setbacks. Even the most prepared students encounter disappointments. A poor grade on an exam. A roommate conflict. Financial aid confusion. A rejection letter from an internship.

Students who lack resilience often interpret these setbacks as signs of failure. They spiral into self-doubt, disengagement, and sometimes withdrawal. Students who have resilience, on the other hand, view setbacks as temporary. They learn from them, adjust their strategies, and move forward.

The difference is not intelligence or talent. It is perspective.

Resilient students understand that success is not defined by avoiding failure but by what they do after failure happens.

Stories of Resilience

- **The Academic Comeback:** David failed his first chemistry exam and considered changing majors. With tutoring, office hours, and steady effort, he improved his grades and eventually earned a degree in biochemistry. His resilience turned an early failure into long-term success.
- **The Financial Struggle:** Simone faced an unexpected tuition gap mid-semester. Instead of withdrawing quietly, she reached out to the financial aid office, applied for scholarships, and spoke with her professors. Her proactive response allowed her to continue her studies.
- **The Personal Loss:** Enrique lost his grandmother during finals week. Grief overwhelmed him, but he sought support from his campus ministry and counseling center. By processing his loss rather than suppressing it, he was able to return to his studies with renewed focus.

These stories remind us that resilience does not erase difficulty. It transforms it into growth.

How Students Can Build Resilience

Resilience is a skill that students can develop intentionally. Some strategies include:

- **Reframing Failure:** Instead of seeing setbacks as permanent, resilient students view them as

opportunities to learn. A failed test becomes feedback, not a final verdict.
- **Seeking Support:** Resilient students do not isolate themselves. They reach out to friends, mentors, or counselors when challenges arise.
- **Developing Problem-Solving Skills:** They break down challenges into manageable steps rather than becoming overwhelmed by the whole.
- **Practicing Self-Care:** Adequate sleep, nutrition, and exercise provide the physical foundation for resilience.
- **Maintaining Perspective:** Resilient students remember their long-term goals and keep setbacks in context.

One student, Clara, kept a journal of challenges and responses. Each time she overcame a difficulty, she recorded how she did it. Over time, she created a personal resilience playbook that reminded her she had the tools to keep going.

The Role of Families

Families can nurture resilience by offering both support and perspective. Too often, parents rush to solve every problem for their student. While well-intentioned, this can unintentionally prevent students from learning problem-solving skills.

Instead, families can ask guiding questions. "What options have you considered?" "Who on campus could help you with this?" These questions encourage students to take ownership while still feeling supported.

Families can also model resilience by sharing their own stories of overcoming challenges. When students see resilience in action at home, they are more likely to practice it themselves.

. . .

Institutional Responsibility

Colleges and universities have a responsibility to create environments where resilience is possible. Institutions that are rigid, unsupportive, or unclear in communication can crush even the most determined students.

The best campuses offer multiple support services, including counseling, tutoring, mentoring, and financial aid guidance, and communicate them clearly. They train faculty to recognize signs of student struggle and respond with empathy. They design policies with flexibility, such as allowing course withdrawals without penalty or offering incomplete grades in times of crisis.

One institution I visited created a resilience-building program for first-year students. The program taught stress management, problem-solving, and coping strategies. Students who participated reported higher confidence and persistence. Resilience was not left to chance. It was cultivated.

From Surviving to Thriving

Resilience is often framed as survival, as if it's only about getting through tough times. But true resilience goes further. It transforms challenges into opportunities for growth, leading students not just to survive but to thrive.

Students who thrive do not merely recover from setbacks. They emerge stronger, wiser, and more confident. Their resilience becomes part of their identity, preparing them not only for college but for life.

When resilience is nurtured, college becomes more than an academic journey. It becomes a training ground for life's inevitable challenges.

Closing Reflections

Every student will face difficulties in college. Some will stumble, some will stall, and some will rise. The difference is resilience. Students who build resilience persist to graduation, families who encourage it provide lasting support, and institutions that foster it create graduates prepared for both careers and life.

Resilience is not about avoiding the storm. It is about learning to walk through it without losing direction. With resilience, students do more than survive college. They thrive in it, and because of it.

Reflection and Practice
For Students

1. Think of a recent challenge. How did you respond? What would resilience look like in that situation?
2. List three campus resources you can turn to when facing difficulties.
3. Identify one habit you can develop that will strengthen your resilience this semester.

For Families

1. Reflect on how you respond when your student faces challenges. Do you solve the problem for them or guide them through it?
2. Share a personal story of resilience with your student this week.
3. Ask your student how they define resilience and what it means to them.

For Institutions

1. Do your policies and practices support or stifle student resilience?

2. How are you training faculty and staff to recognize and respond to student struggles?
3. What programs or workshops could you create to build resilience skills in first-year students?

Practice Steps

- **Students:** Keep a resilience journal for one month, recording challenges faced and how you responded.
- **Families:** Replace one "fix it" response with a guiding question the next time your student shares a problem.
- **Institutions:** Launch one initiative this year that explicitly teaches resilience skills to students.

Chapter Ten

THE GRADUATION GAP: WHY PERSISTENCE MATTERS MORE THAN ENROLLMENT

The Graduation Gap: Why Persistence Matters More Than Enrollment

Starting Strong Is Not Enough

Every fall, college campuses burst with energy. Families unload cars filled with clothes, mini-fridges, and dreams. Students step onto campus eager to begin a new chapter. For institutions, these scenes are proof of successful recruitment. Enrollment numbers are celebrated, and press releases boast of record incoming classes.

But behind the excitement lies a sobering reality. For too many students, the journey that begins with move-in day never ends with graduation. Nationally, only about five out of ten students who start college finish with a degree. At some institutions, the numbers are even lower.

I remember meeting a student named Christopher during his first week on campus. He was full of ambition and determination. Yet by his third semester, financial struggles and academic challenges pushed him to leave. He became part of the silent majority of students who enroll but never finish.

Enrollment is important, but it is only the beginning. The true measure of higher education is not how many students start, but how many persist to the finish line. In this chapter, we will explore why persistence matters more than enrollment, what barriers stand in the way, and how students, families, and institutions can work together to close the graduation gap.

The Illusion of Enrollment Success

Colleges often measure their success by the number of students they attract. High enrollment numbers bring in tuition dollars, improve rankings, and create positive headlines. But focusing on enrollment alone can create an illusion of success.

If a university enrolls one thousand students but graduates only five hundred, has it truly fulfilled its mission? Recruitment without persistence is like starting a marathon with a large crowd, but watching half of them drop out before the finish line.

Families, too, sometimes fall into this trap. Parents beam with pride when their child enrolls, believing the most challenging part is over. But enrollment is only the first hurdle. The real test is persistence. The real test is continuing through the inevitable challenges until the degree is earned.

Barriers to Persistence

Persistence is not a matter of willpower alone. Students face real barriers that make completing a degree difficult.

- **Financial Strain:** Tuition increases, gaps in aid, and unexpected costs derail many students. Even small balances can block registration and force withdrawals.
- **Academic Preparedness:** Some students arrive underprepared for college-level work. Without support, they quickly fall behind and lose confidence.

- **Mental Health Challenges:** Anxiety, depression, and stress undermine persistence when students do not have adequate support.
- **Family Obligations:** Caring for siblings, working long hours, or supporting family members can pull students away from their academics.
- **Institutional Barriers:** Complicated policies, lack of advising, and poor communication make it difficult for students to navigate the system.

I once worked with a student named Tasha who was thriving academically but suddenly had to care for her younger brother when her mother passed away. Without flexible policies or additional support, she dropped out of school. Her departure had nothing to do with ability. It was about circumstances.

Stories of Persistence

Persistence comes alive in the stories of students who overcame obstacles.

- **The Financial Fighter:** Jeanelle faced a two-thousand-dollar balance that threatened to end her education. Instead of giving up, she sought scholarships, met with financial aid staff, and negotiated a payment plan. She graduated on time.
- **The Academic Comeback:** Alisha failed her first math course but refused to let it define her. She enrolled in tutoring, met regularly with her professor, and passed the course the second time. Her persistence carried her through to a degree in education.
- **The Support Seeker:** Daniella battled depression that nearly caused her to withdraw. By reaching out to counseling services and leaning on her friends, she

regained stability. Her persistence was measured not just in the classes she completed but in the courage she sustained.

These stories remind us that persistence is not about smooth sailing. It is about navigating storms with determination and support.

Why Persistence Matters

Persistence matters because without it, enrollment means little. Students who leave college without a degree often carry debt but no credential, creating financial strain without the benefit of improved career opportunities.

For families, persistence is the fulfillment of dreams and the sacrifices that come with them. Parents who work multiple jobs or make financial sacrifices want to see their children cross the finish line. Enrollment honors their hopes. Graduation honors their sacrifices.

For institutions, persistence reflects the integrity of their mission. Colleges exist not just to admit students but to educate and graduate them. Retention and graduation rates reveal whether institutions are truly serving their students.

Strategies for Students

Students can strengthen persistence by embracing strategies that prepare them for challenges.

- **Seek Support Early:** Whether academic or financial, problems grow if ignored. Asking for help at the first sign of trouble prevents crises.
- **Build a Network:** Mentors, friends, and advisors provide encouragement and accountability.

- **Stay Focused on Long-Term Goals:** Remembering why you started can fuel persistence when short-term struggles arise.
- **Balance Work and Study:** Limit work hours to protect academic progress.
- **Prioritize Well-Being:** Physical and mental health sustain the energy required for persistence.

One student I worked with, Chanel, carried a photo of her grandmother in her backpack. Each time she thought of giving up, she looked at it and reminded herself of the sacrifices made for her education. That reminder gave her the strength to persist.

The Role of Families

Families are critical partners in persistence. Encouragement, perspective, and accountability from home can keep students moving forward when they are tempted to stop.

Families can:

- Celebrate progress, not just milestones.
- Ask open-ended questions that invite honesty, such as "What challenges are you facing this week?"
- Provide perspective by reminding students of long-term goals.
- Support financially when possible, even with small contributions that cover books or transportation.

Families should avoid assuming silence means success. Regular check-ins help uncover struggles before they become insurmountable.

Institutional Responsibility

Institutions have a moral and strategic obligation to prioritize persistence. Policies, programs, and support services must be designed with completion in mind. Some effective approaches include:

- **Proactive Advising:** Advisors who reach out to students regularly instead of waiting for problems.
- **Financial Safety Nets:** Emergency aid and flexible payment plans that prevent small balances from ending a student's journey.
- **Academic Support:** Tutoring, supplemental instruction, and writing centers and math labs that address skill gaps.
- **Wellness Services:** Counseling and health programs that sustain student well-being.
- **Community Building:** Programs that foster belonging, especially for first-generation or underrepresented students.

One university I observed in Atlanta, GA, created a fund that provided small grants to seniors with outstanding balances. The result was a significant increase in graduation rates. The investment was modest. The impact was profound.

Closing Reflections

Enrollment opens the door, but persistence walks through it. A college education is not measured by how many students start, but by how many finish. Students who persist gain more than degrees. They gain resilience, confidence, and opportunity.

Families who encourage persistence help students transform dreams into reality. Institutions that prioritize persistence prove their commitment to student success.

The graduation gap is not inevitable. With support, strategy, and determination, students can move from the excitement of enrollment to the triumph of graduation. Persistence is the bridge. Without it, enrollment is a promise unfulfilled. With it, education becomes transformation.

Reflection and Practice
For Students

1. Reflect on your "why." What long-term goals will keep you motivated when challenges arise?
2. Identify three campus resources you can use to support persistence.
3. What small habits will you commit to that will strengthen your focus and discipline?

For Families

1. How often do you check in with your student about challenges, not just successes?
2. What sacrifices have you made for their education, and how can you share those stories as encouragement?
3. How can you celebrate persistence at each stage, not just at graduation?

For Institutions

1. What is your current retention and graduation rate, and how does it reflect your mission?
2. What safety nets do you provide to prevent small financial or academic challenges from ending a student's journey?
3. How are you building cultures of belonging that keep students engaged and motivated?

Institutions have a moral and strategic obligation to prioritize persistence. Policies, programs, and support services must be designed with completion in mind.

Some effective approaches include:

- **Proactive Advising:** Advisors who reach out to students regularly instead of waiting for problems.
- **Financial Safety Nets:** Emergency aid and flexible payment plans that prevent small balances from ending a student's journey.
- **Academic Support:** Tutoring, supplemental instruction, and writing centers and math labs that address skill gaps.
- **Wellness Services:** Counseling and health programs that sustain student well-being.
- **Community Building:** Programs that foster belonging, especially for first-generation or underrepresented students.

One university I observed in Atlanta, GA, created a fund that provided small grants to seniors with outstanding balances. The result was a significant increase in graduation rates. The investment was modest. The impact was profound.

Closing Reflections

Enrollment opens the door, but persistence walks through it. A college education is not measured by how many students start, but by how many finish. Students who persist gain more than degrees. They gain resilience, confidence, and opportunity.

Families who encourage persistence help students transform dreams into reality. Institutions that prioritize persistence prove their commitment to student success.

The graduation gap is not inevitable. With support, strategy, and determination, students can move from the excitement of enrollment to the triumph of graduation. Persistence is the bridge. Without it, enrollment is a promise unfulfilled. With it, education becomes transformation.

Reflection and Practice
For Students

1. Reflect on your "why." What long-term goals will keep you motivated when challenges arise?
2. Identify three campus resources you can use to support persistence.
3. What small habits will you commit to that will strengthen your focus and discipline?

For Families

1. How often do you check in with your student about challenges, not just successes?
2. What sacrifices have you made for their education, and how can you share those stories as encouragement?
3. How can you celebrate persistence at each stage, not just at graduation?

For Institutions

1. What is your current retention and graduation rate, and how does it reflect your mission?
2. What safety nets do you provide to prevent small financial or academic challenges from ending a student's journey?
3. How are you building cultures of belonging that keep students engaged and motivated?

Practice Steps

- **Students:** Write down your graduation date and place it somewhere visible as a daily reminder of your goal.
- **Families:** Begin a monthly check-in with your student to talk specifically about persistence.
- **Institutions:** Develop one new initiative this year that directly targets graduation rates, such as a completion grant or proactive advising program.

Chapter Eleven

EDUCATION AS TRANSFORMATION: BEYOND THE DEGREE

Education as Transformation: Beyond the Degree

The End That is Really a Beginning

Graduation day is often painted as the end of a journey. Students walk across a stage, families cheer, institutions boast of another successful class. Yet if you listen closely on that day, you realize that graduation is less of a conclusion and more of a launching point. The real story of education is not just about crossing a stage, but about what happens afterward. Lives changed, communities uplifted, and habits carried forward.

When I began writing this book, my goal was not simply to provide a roadmap to college completion. It was to explore the more profound truth that education is a transformative process. It reshapes students into thinkers, leaders, and contributors. It empowers families to see possibilities where there was once only struggle. It challenges institutions to fulfill their highest calling: not simply to enroll and collect tuition, but to guide, nurture, and persist with students until the very end.

As we close this book together, I want to revisit the journey we have taken, draw out the larger lessons, and offer a challenge to everyone invested in education. This chapter is about taking a step back to see the whole picture. We must see the story of persistence as the thread that holds everything together.

The Arc of the Journey

This book has unfolded in four natural movements, each representing a distinct stage of the college journey.

Laying the Foundation (Chapters 1–3)

We began by looking at the earliest days of college. The first ninety days, the value of scholarship dollars, and the power of building networks all represented foundational moves. These were not glamorous topics, but they were critical. Students who take the time to adjust academically, manage their money wisely, and form supportive relationships build a strong base for everything that follows. Without a foundation, the house collapses. Without these practices, persistence falters.

Growing Skills and Balance (Chapters 4–6)

Next, we turned to growth. Students learned to lead without titles, to navigate financial realities beyond scholarships, and to balance work commitments with academic success. These chapters reminded us that college is not simply about being taught, but about developing skills. Leadership, self-management, and balance are qualities that prepare students not just for coursework, but for life. This section of the journey demanded maturity. It called on students to move beyond surviving into intentional growth.

Sustaining Success (Chapters 7–9)

The third movement acknowledged the storms students inevitably face. Mental health challenges, the demands of experiential learning, and the need for resilience all test persistence. Sustaining success is about more than grit; it is about building systems of care, leaning on networks, and practicing balance when the excitement of the early days wears off. Here, the themes shifted from external actions to internal strength.

Sustaining success is about enduring, and in many ways, it is the most difficult stage of all.

Reaching the Outcome (Chapter 10)

Finally, we arrived at the truth that enrollment means little without persistence. The graduation gap is real, and the true mission of higher education must be measured not in how many students start, but in how many finish. This final movement brought us to the heart of the matter. Persistence is the bridge. Graduation is the measure. Without persistence, education is a broken promise. With persistence, it becomes transformational.

Stories That Carry Us Forward

Throughout these chapters, we encountered students who taught us what persistence looks like in real life.

There was Christopher, whose ambition at the start of his journey gave way to financial stress that forced him to leave. His story reminded us that enrollment is only the beginning.

There was Tasha, who left school not because she lacked talent, but because family responsibilities overtook her. She reminded us that circumstances often matter more than capability.

There was Jeanelle, who faced a seemingly insurmountable balance but fought through with creativity and support. Her persistence earned her a degree and a future.

There was Chanel, who carried her grandmother's photo as a reminder of the sacrifices behind her education. Her story revealed that persistence is sometimes rooted in love and memory more than in ambition.

And there was Daniella, who confronted depression and found stability by seeking help. Her story reminded us that mental health is not an afterthought, but central to persistence.

These students, and countless others like them, are why we write, teach, and build programs. They remind us that persistence is not abstract. It is deeply human. It is about students making choices in the midst of pressure, families offering encouragement when exhaustion sets in, and institutions designing pathways that keep doors open.

Beyond the Degree

If there is one message I want readers to carry forward, it is this: graduation is not the final goal. Transformation is.

For students, the lessons of persistence extend far beyond college walls. The habits developed here, like time management, financial responsibility, networking, resilience, and wellness, will serve you in careers, relationships, and communities. The degree you hang on your wall is not just a receipt to prove you paid for college. It is evidence that you can face challenges, adapt, and continue. Those are life skills, not just college skills.

For families, the sacrifices you make and the encouragement you give ripple outward. Your support does not end on graduation day. It continues as you guide your students into adulthood, model persistence in your own lives, and inspire future generations.

For institutions, graduation is not the finish line either. Your true measure is in the students you help shape, the leaders you help launch, and the communities you strengthen through the graduates you have nurtured. Higher education is not simply about producing employees for the workforce. It is about forming whole people who will shape the future.

A Call to Students

To the students reading this: know that persistence is your superpower. You will face setbacks. You will be tempted to quit. But you are capable of more than you imagine. Every class you pass, every obstacle you overcome, and every resource you seek out strengthens you. Remember that education is not a race against others. It is a journey of growth within yourself.

Carry forward the networks you built. Continue to practice financial wisdom. Protect your mental health. Believe in the vision of yourself not just as a graduate, but as a contributor to the world. Let your degree be a launching pad, not a resting place.

A Call to Families

To the families: your role is irreplaceable. The encouragement you give, the perspective you share, and the sacrifices you make matter more than you may ever know. Students may not always say thank you, but they carry your support with them into every classroom and every challenge.

Continue to check in. Continue to remind your students of their worth. Continue to celebrate small steps, not just milestones. Education is not just about producing graduates. It is about producing resilient, grounded people who know they are not alone.

A Call to Institutions

To the institutions: you must measure your success not by how many students you recruit, but by how many you graduate. Retention programs, emergency aid, proactive advising, mental health services, and intentional community-building are not luxuries. They are necessities. They are the infrastructure of persistence.

Examine your policies. Ask whether they are creating opportunities or erecting barriers. Listen to student voices. Adapt your models. Invest in completion as intentionally as you invest in recruitment. Your legacy will be measured in degrees completed and lives transformed, not in enrollment numbers alone.

The Power of Hope

At its heart, education is an act of hope. Every student who enrolls is making a declaration of belief in their own future. Every family who invests is making a declaration of belief in possibility. Every institution that opens its doors is making a declaration of belief in transformation.

Persistence is how we honor that hope. It is how we turn possibility into reality.

Graduation is not the end. It is the visible marker of an invisible journey. It is a journey of resilience, sacrifice, and growth. It is proof that persistence wins.

Closing Vision

As we close this book, I want to leave you with this truth: education is more than a degree. It is transformation. It is the process of becoming. It is the journey from uncertainty to confidence, from potential to purpose, from enrollment to impact.

Students, keep persisting. Families, keep supporting. Institutions, keep reforming. Together, we can close the graduation gap. Together, we can honor the sacrifices, the dreams, and the hopes tied to every enrollment form and every tuition bill.

The journey is not over at graduation. It is just beginning.

Education is persistence. Education is transformation. Education is life.

Chapter Twelve

STUDY GUIDE: DISCUSSION AND REFLECTION QUESTIONS

Study Guide: Discussion and Reflection Questions
This Study Guide is designed to help students, families, and institutions reflect on the lessons of Thriving in College. Use these additional questions for personal reflection, family conversations, mentoring sessions, or group discussions. Each set of questions corresponds to a single chapter and encourages the practical application of the ideas presented.

CHAPTER 1 – THE FIRST 90 DAYS OF COLLEGE

- What specific steps can you take in your first 90 days to feel connected to your campus?
- How do small daily habits (study time, sleep, exercise) shape your success?
- What does "belonging" mean to you in a college setting, and how will you find it?
- When challenges arise early, how will you respond instead of retreating?
- Who can you identify as a mentor, advisor, or peer to guide your transition?

CHAPTER 2 – MAKING EVERY DOLLAR COUNT

- How do you view scholarships: as an end goal or as part of a bigger financial plan?
- Do you know whether your scholarship is renewable? What steps will you take to keep it?
- If you receive a refund check, how would you budget it across the semester?
- What hidden or unexpected costs of college should you prepare for?
- How can you balance scholarships, grants, and loans to avoid unnecessary debt?

CHAPTER 3 – BUILDING A SUPPORT NETWORK

- Who are three people you can turn to right now for academic, social, or emotional support?
- How can you tell the difference between positive and negative influences in your circle?
- What does accountability look like for you, and who can provide it?
- How can you expand your network beyond friends to include professors or professionals?
- What role does reciprocity (giving as well as receiving) play in building a strong network?

CHAPTER 4 – LEADING WITHOUT TITLES

- How can you demonstrate leadership in everyday actions without an official position?
- What opportunities on campus allow you to lead informally or through service?

- How does serving others strengthen your leadership skills?
- Think of a leader you admire. What qualities do they display that you can practice?
- How will you measure your own growth as a leader throughout college?

CHAPTER 5 – BEYOND SCHOLARSHIPS: UNDERSTANDING AID REALITIES

- Do you clearly understand the difference between scholarships, grants, loans, and work-study?
- What questions should you ask a financial aid officer to fully understand your package?
- What does "borrowing wisely" mean to you in practical terms?
- How can you prepare now to reapply for scholarships each year of college?
- What would you do differently if you discovered that one of your scholarships was nonrenewable?

CHAPTER 6 – BALANCING WORK, LIFE, AND ACADEMICS

- How many hours per week can you realistically work without harming your studies?
- What strategies can you use to balance time between study, work, and social life?
- What signals might tell you that your balance is slipping, and how will you respond?
- How can you use scheduling or planning tools to stay in control of your commitments?
- What does it mean to you to practice "balance" as a skill, not just a state of being?

CHAPTER 7 – MENTAL HEALTH AND WELLNESS IN COLLEGE

- What are your personal warning signs of stress, anxiety, or burnout?
- Where on campus can you go for mental health or wellness support?
- How do you personally define wellness, and what practices help you maintain it?
- What role do friends, family, and mentors play in supporting your mental health?
- How can you normalize conversations about mental health in your own circles?

CHAPTER 8 – EXPERIENTIAL LEARNING AND CAREER PREPARATION

- Why is experiential learning (internships, volunteering, research) important to you?
- What opportunities on your campus could provide career-related experience?
- How can you turn setbacks in internships or jobs into learning opportunities?
- Who can help connect you to professional or career-building opportunities?
- How does gaining real-world experience while in school impact your confidence?

CHAPTER 9 – BUILDING RESILIENCE

- Think of a time you failed or faced a setback. What did you learn from it?
- How do peers, family, or mentors help you bounce back from challenges?

- What role does resilience play in persistence through college?
- How can you reframe obstacles as opportunities for growth?
- What strategies will you use to build resilience when life feels overwhelming?

CHAPTER 10 – PERSISTENCE AND GRADUATION

- What does persistence mean to you in your college journey?
- Why do so many students leave college before finishing, and what could change that?
- What habits or practices will carry you all the way to graduation?
- How do you imagine celebrating graduation with your family and community?
- What will your degree represent to you beyond the credential itself?

CHAPTER 11 – EDUCATION AS TRANSFORMATION

- How has your view of college shifted after reading this book?
- Which lessons from these chapters will you carry with you beyond college?
- How can you apply persistence and resilience to other areas of your life?
- In what ways can you support others in their own educational journey?
- What does it mean to see education not just as a degree, but as transformation?

ABOUT THE AUTHOR

Rasheem Rooke is a nonprofit leader, author, and educator committed to expanding access to higher education and helping students not only enroll, but graduate and thrive.

As Assistant Vice President of Program Management at UNCF, he oversees hundreds of scholarships and programs that award tens of millions of dollars each year. His work bridges universities, donors, and families, addressing the real challenges of student success, from financial need to emergency aid to the systems that sustain persistence.

Beyond his professional leadership, Rasheem is a spoken word artist, photographer, storyteller, and the author of two suspense novels. He also develops resources for aspiring writers, combining his passion for equity and resilience with creativity and transformation.

Through books, speaking, and program development, he has inspired students, families, and institutions to think differently about what it truly takes to succeed in college. Thriving in College: Ten Real World Lessons for College Success distills years of experience and student stories into a practical guide for anyone invested in education.

He believes that persistence, in college and in life, changes everything.

instagram.com/officiallyrasheem
facebook.com/rasheem.rooke
tiktok.com/officiallyrasheem

ALSO BY RASHEEM ROOKE

Enjoy these works of fiction by the author.

Black Ribisi

Broken Brotherhood

www.ingramcontent.com/pod-product-compliance
Lightning Source LLC
Chambersburg PA
CBHW052207090526
44583CB00017BA/2410